Life as I knew it

Melissa L. Gomez

Copyright © 2024

All rights reserved.

ISBN:

All rights reserved. No part of this publication may be reproduced, distributed, or transmitted in any form or by any means, including photocopying, recording, or other electronic or mechanical methods, without the author's prior written permission, except in the case of brief quotations embodied in critical reviews and certain other non-commercial uses permitted by copyright law. For permission requests, please get in touch with the author.

Table of Contents

Dedication i
About the Author ii
Chapter 1 1
Chapter 2 4
Chapter 3 6
Chapter 4 12
Chapter 5 18

Dedication

This book is dedicated to my late mother, for whom without I would never have learned resilience.

About the Author

Melissa was raised in Queens, NY, by her single mom and older sister. She had a passion for writing from an early age and was able to dive deeper into that passion once admitted to a creative writing program in high school. She continued to explore her passion for writing in her college studies by taking several English and writing courses. She writes from real-life experiences and hopes to inspire others through whatever adversities they may face.

Chapter 1

Do you ever wonder why we lie to little kids? Ever thought seriously about what we fill their heads up with? Little kids believe in all these fairytales, and to make matters worse, society really plays it up. There are all these holidays where magical creatures bring you presents. It's so misleading; we go through childhood thinking the world is a wonderful place. We believe there are fairy godmothers, princes, and princesses; only to wake up one day and realize it's all been a lie. Life, in fact, isn't always so good - there's crime and heartache, and people don't live forever. People get hurt, people get sick, and sadly enough, there is no fairy godmother to grant them good health. Unluckily enough for me, there was no fairy godmother to make this better for her. Surely at the time, I was way passed believing in fairytales, but I had yet to discover how cold of a world we really lived in. So like a train I wasn't expecting, the news of what I was about to be told completely blew me off from the platform I so firmly stood on most of my life. My mom had a tumor in her lung; it was all said so nonchalantly, *"It's a simple fix; I will take off a few months from work and go through some chemo. The doctors are confident that will take care of things."*

An hour earlier, life had been so normal. It was a cloudy

October day; a light chill swept the streets, perfect hoodie weather – the type of weather I warmly embraced. Crystal had come over to do my hair, and we sat in my room as we discussed the latest about our boyfriends. It was the beginning of our senior year, our last year of high school, and while we both knew we were supposed to go through big changes in the year to come, neither of us knew at the time just how much life would change. We both sat there in a daze after my mom had shared the news. *"It just doesn't seem real,"* I said to Crystal after she left the room. *"Well, like your mom said, it's a simple fix"* Crystal seemed so reassured, and since I wanted to be reassured, too, I decided to shift my focus back to my social life.

Friday evenings were always an adventure for us, Crystal and I met in the 8th grade and had been inseparable ever since. My house was her house, and her house was mine, so if anybody could convince me things were going to be okay, it was her. Our friend Sam was throwing one of his usual parties, so we decided to head out and get our weekend started. When we arrived at Sam's, his garage was already packed with some other people he'd invited, the music was bumping, and Sam had used his fake ID to stock up on tons of liquor. *"Hey! What do you girls want to drink?"* Sam asked as he happily greeted us. Eager to be distracted by the recent news I'd received about my mom and hoping Sam's energy would rub off on me, *"I'll have whatever you're having,"* I responded. I began sipping and slowly faded away with the night.

Chapter 2

Over the next week, my mom carried on like things were business as usual. She was the strongest person I knew, invincible in my eyes. She decided she needed to go to the salon because, of course, she couldn't go through her 'vacation' from work without looking her best. But once her nails and hair were perfectly done, we were about to find out how far away we actually were from *"a simple fix."* She got into her car to drive off, but before she could leave, her first seizure took over. Thankfully one of the girls inside the hair salon saw her and was able to call an ambulance to assist.

News of her seizure made its way to me as I was out with Crystal and her family. Reality was shifting faster than my brain could even adjust, and walking into the emergency room to visit her was surreal. Turns out, she didn't just have a tumor in her lung; the tumor had traveled to her brain, wrapping around it. Despite us not knowing, the tumor had been growing for months and just now decided to strike. *"You don't have to worry about a thing; you'll see the best doctors, and get the best care in NYU hospital,"* Edna, whose brother was a doctor at NYU, decided to offer. Edna was a family friend from my mom's childhood neighborhood, they didn't see each other regularly, but when Crystal and I arrived, she was already by my mom's bedside with my uncle's wife, Stacy. While I was still trying to wrap my head around what was happening, Edna and Stacy already seemed to have things planned out. Crystal's parents told my mom I could stay with them, so she could focus on getting better. I was happy I'd be with Crystal, but I found it very odd how swiftly Edna and Stacy volunteered when we hadn't seen them very regularly over the years.

Chapter 3

Maybe it was the tumor, maybe it was the shock, but my mom was convinced I was bad for her health. She told me I gave her cancer as though cancer could be spread like the common cold. She said she couldn't deal with me and completely shut me out. My many calls and attempts to reach her went unanswered. I had slept at Crystal's countless times before, but knowing I was no longer welcomed at home weighed on my mind, and racing thoughts made a good night's rest nearly impossible.

As the weeks passed, Thanksgiving day arrived. Crystal's parents told us we could have a mini get-together, so we invited Sam and Lucas over (Lucas had been my boyfriend since sophomore year of high school.) The four of us snuck down wine coolers to the basement to begin our little party. A couple wine coolers in, and the drama that had plagued my life over the last few weeks seemed to dissipate; it seemed that a little alcohol buzz was just the thing needed to distract me for the moment. The feelings of rejection that consumed my mind over the last few weeks, from my mom refusing to take or return my calls, were finally pushed to the back of my mind. We were all having a good time, laughing and smiling. I absentmindedly stumbled to the bathroom, and as I took off my jeans to use the bathroom, my cell phone popped out of my back pocket and flew straight into the toilet bowl. FML, there goes my phone, I thought.

The next morning, my phone still wouldn't turn on. I called my mom a bunch of times to try to see if there was something that could be done or if it was a total loss. When I finally got through to her, she was furious with me. *"I'm coming to get you; you're coming home immediately,"* she adamantly said to me. I was beyond confused, she wouldn't speak to me for the last two months, but suddenly I had to urgently return home. She got to Crystal's before I could even finish packing; as she waited in the living room for me to get ready, she could be overheard on the phone. *"She can drown in a lake at this point for all I care,"* referring to me. Crystal's family hesitantly said their goodbyes to me as we made our way outside to the car.

Edna and Stacy were waiting right in front of our house for us to return. As soon as I got out of the car, they both jumped in front of me, *"Now you listen, you are going to go to Virginia tomorrow, and you aren't giving your mother any issues about it,"* they threatened. Me going to Virginia was news to me. It now made sense why I had to return home urgently out of nowhere. After a couple of months of being discarded, now they wanted me completely shipped off. Walking into what for so long used to be my home now seemed like a sort of prison. I was not allowed to touch the house phone or the computers - they didn't want me to contact anybody to say goodbye or form an escape plan, I guess. Purely under the influence of Edna and Stacy, my mom was enforcing all of these restrictions with an iron fist.

Later in the evening, once Edna and Stacy had left, I convinced my mom to let me use her laptop. Escape plan was in full effect; if I was getting dragged out of New York, it was going to be with my fists swinging. I instant messaged Lucas, letting him know what was going on. Given that Lucas had been trying to convince me to move in with him for the last two years, he was eager to help me run away.

Once my mom went to bed for the night, I climbed out onto the roof underneath my bedroom window. Slowly and quietly as possible, I handed Lucas my suitcase. I jumped down, and we hurried off to the train station to head back to his place. I put my hoodie up and had my scarf covering most of my face; we didn't want any video footage to facially recognize me or to be able to track where I went.

Within two weeks, my older sister Jane found me on social media, *"Mom just wants to know if you are okay; she called the police, and they told her this is NYC & with all the 17-year-olds missing, there isn't anything they would be able to do."* Turned out that even without legal emancipation, I didn't have to hide.

My mom was in NYU hospital, under Edna's brother's wing. They were conducting her Chemotherapy and administering all types of medication. I had bounced around so much that with all the schoolwork missed, I was behind and didn't know how to catch up. So instead of going to school, I went to NYU to see her daily. I'd get there early and sit in her room. She was there physically, but the tumor had taken her mentally. Edna and Stacy would come in sporadically, as would my uncles, then they would take food breaks. And I would stay in my mom's room all day, a teenager who had never worked a day in her life - a teen without two dimes to rub together. But they all considered me problematic, and they all considered me to be somebody else's problem. I sat in that room religiously, on the window sill overlooking Manhattan. At night I would cry myself to sleep, uncomfortable and hungry. My life had changed as I'd known it, and my mom wasn't there to ask for help anymore.

"Your mom is going to die any day now, so we are going to pack up her belongings in her apartment," Edna and Stacy told Jane and me when we arrived at the hospital that day. We looked at each other in disbelief; our intuition told us something was off about Edna and Stacy. But our mom had put so much trust into them helping through her cancer. We took what they said with a grain of salt. In private, we tried to devise a plan of how to stop them from emptying out her

apartment. We decided to go to my mom's landlord and tell her our concerns; Edna and Stacy had the keys to her apartment; so with the landlord's help, we had the locks changed to keep them out. We didn't know exactly what they were up to, but something in our gut told us they were up to no good.

The next day Edna and Stacy were furious. When I arrived at the hospital, a social worker asked me to accompany him into another room to discuss urgent matters. *"As per your mother's request, a list has been made. This list restricts visits from your father's side of the family, including you and your sister, for urgent health matters. Your mother has more seizures when you are here, and it is for her best interest that you all no longer visit."* I sat there in disbelief hearing this, but I went into my mom's room anyway to say goodbye. *"You need to leave now,"* Edna snapped at me, *"I'm going to call security."* I ignored Edna and sat on my mom's bedside, warning her, *"Mom listen to me - you can't trust them; they're up to something."* She was actually awake for once, but still couldn't quite see eye to eye with me. The security guard came in to tell me I had to leave so not to be forcibly removed; I walked out.

Christmas was quickly approaching, and while visiting Crystal's, I decided to bake some chocolate chip cookies to put together in a mini wicker basket. I wrapped the cookies in festive plastic bags, stuck them in the basket with a card, and dropped the basket off at my mom's front door. She was supposed to have been back home from her treatments, but unbeknown to me, she wasn't around. During a call, Stacy told my sister, *"I'm inviting your mother over to my place for Christmas so that Marissa can be alone."* Disturbed and concerned, Jane relayed the message to me shortly after. The malicious comments convinced us they were definitely up to no good.

Once the new year came, my mom was scheduled to head back to NYU for another round of chemo, and since neither Jane nor I were allowed to see her in the hospital anymore, we asked an old family friend to visit. To our surprise, arriving at the front desk, our friend was told our mom was no longer a patient there. We had no idea what happened; we didn't know how that could be possible. To our knowledge, she was still receiving cancer treatments there. But Edna and Stacy had completely pushed us out now. My mom was unreachable; we couldn't find her. We couldn't be there for her. She couldn't be there for us.

I wondered why I was allowed to believe lies as a little kid. I wondered why I was led to believe in fairytales… Fairytales didn't prepare us for this.

Chapter 4

Conditioning allows us to believe in the way things should be. We are raised to believe there's a proper process to follow. Go to school, get good grades, go to college, get a degree, get a 'good' job, marry, buy a house with the white picket fence, and have kids. They have us sold on this process before we can even figure out who we want to be. But life doesn't always go according to plan, does it?

"You are acing these practice tests; why don't you just finish out what you have left of high school?" My GED instructor just didn't get it. And why would he? I was only 17, quick-witted, and my exterior could never accurately display the internal trainwreck inside of me. I still appeared well put together, in pretty clean clothes my mom had got me, and smiling as if nothing had ever changed. Lacking a steady home and being unwanted was the last thought that came to mind when strangers saw me. Completing this program was one of many steps I laid out for myself for me to become independent and self-sufficient. As I handed in the last of my work, the school day was over for me. I walked outside of the campus into the warm Virginia air. I stood outside as I awaited a ride from my dad.

I hadn't seen my dad frequently over the recent years. Before I made it to middle school he relocated from NYC to

Virginia and remarried. My dad's wife was significantly younger than him and not much of a fan of my presence in their home. Although my dad ignored her complaints, it wasn't so easy for me to stomach doing the same.

"My official GED exam is scheduled for next week, and once I pass, I am heading back to New York," I told my dad as I got into his car. *"Okay, honey,"* was the nonchalant reply he offered. I came down to his house two weeks prior; there wasn't much I could do in New York at the time, given the mess I had left behind. All I wanted was to go back with my GED finished so that I could start college and get a job to support myself. My mom hadn't spoken to me in months, I had no idea where she was, and to my knowledge, Jane hadn't had contact with her either. Although we were worried, in all honesty, we were also kind of relieved. Edna and Stacy had repeatedly called us on 3-way during the winter months, *"Why are you so selfish? You don't care about your mother; all you care about is yourself."* The disappearance of their harassment let us breathe easier. My mom had unknowingly turned to the devil for help, and the devil certainly didn't want witnesses.

Lucas wasn't exactly thrilled about me running down south. But I had to focus on setting my future up. Our relationship certainly wouldn't pay the bills. Once his sister had fabricated a story about catching me downtown kissing some other guy, that was my cue to get the heck out of there. Especially considering Lucas had a momentary lapse where he wasn't quite sure what to believe. That was about enough time for me to make arrangements to leave. So here I was down in Virginia, following my mom's original plan for me to go to my dad's. My mom knew I never wanted to be here, but I guess she also knew it would have been the most stable environment for me at the time.

Exam day came, and sure enough, I aced the test with flying colors. In and out of the GED program, within less than a month, I managed to graduate before my actual anticipated graduation date of high school back in New York. With this accomplishment down, I set my sights on returning back to New York. I was going to temporarily stay at my sister's with her husband and my baby niece. Emphasis on temporary; my sister's husband wasn't the biggest fan of having me around. Cultural differences made him concerned that I could be a bad influence on my niece.

When I got off the plane in New York, I was surprised to find not only was Jane there, but my mom was too. Apparently, in my absence, my mom had shown up at Jane's unannounced, wondering where her daughters had been. She hadn't known about the list Edna and Stacy made restricting us from seeing her.

Cancer had taken such a toll on her. It had only been a

few months since I'd last seen her, but even in that short time period, she was no longer the mom I remembered. Before cancer, she was so full of life, youthful even as she aged, an avid gym goer, a dancer even after her long work days at the law firm. But now, she struggled to walk with a cane; she had on a wig to cover up the hair loss the chemo had caused, and the years she previously escaped now showed on her face. But at the least, her warm smile had returned, and her tumor's reign seemed to be over.

Turns out she had been left all alone for months to die in the hospital. Our reunion revealed that the reason we couldn't find her was that Edna had registered her in the hospital again under a false alias. Drugged up and sedated, Edna and Stacy got her to sign over everything in writing to them. Edna took over as her power of attorney. Stacy took over as her healthcare proxy. They had her write a new will leaving both them and my mom's six brothers as sole beneficiaries of her life insurance policy. They drugged my mom up as much as the law would allow and ridiculed her right in front of her face while under sedation, assuming she was too far gone to know. Then when they thought my mom was close to passing, they stopped coming to visit altogether. We listened as our mom told us she would call asking why they weren't visiting, and they would laugh at her and hang up. But to their dismay, she made it through her first round of chemo and rehabilitation. Unluckily for them, our mom didn't die leaving them everything. And she remembered what they had done. Life, as I'd known it seven months earlier, was gone, but we at least got to be our original unit once again.

Being back in New York also meant I got to see Crystal and Lucas again, but not exactly with the same frequency. Under my mom's house rules, I usually had to be home prior to midnight, or if I was sleeping over Crystal's, not at all some nights. But, under my brother-in-law's house rules, I had to be back before 9:00 pm. It wasn't the easiest rule to abide by, but I thought I could make it work. My sister had moved out of NYC when she got married into a house my brother-in-law purchased for them in Long Island. They were close enough to NYC that I could still take public transportation to get around. I was only back for two weeks when the bus I was supposed to take to get back home that night ran late. I was going to end up arriving at 9:30 pm, 30 minutes passed my allotted curfew. In hopes of diffusing the situation, I called my dad, asking if he could talk to my brother-in-law for me. This, unfortunately, had the opposite effect; my brother-in-law was offended by the notion.

My mom got wind of the situation and reached out to me. *"You should move back in with me,"* she told me over a call. I had wanted to go back home since I'd been kicked out, but I was skeptical nonetheless. *"Are you sure you can handle that Mom?"* I asked before agreeing to anything. *"Yes, of course, I'm your mom, and I could use your help here"*. I'd been so wrapped up in bouncing around that it hadn't occurred to me my mom was now limited in her capabilities. I agreed to return home.

I spent the next few weeks making sure housework was taken care of for my mom and food was made. I grew tired of the drama that had surfaced between Lucas and I. Originally, when I came back to NY, I thought he and I could move forward from his sister's made-up story, but he became overbearing and slightly controlling. So in an effort to find peace, I decided to end things between us. My summer now consisted of accompanying my mom to doctor's visits in the daytime and sneaking into clubs at night with my girlfriends. I was back in my element, back in my room, and back to my regular social life. Things seemed as though they were looking up for the better, and I was hopeful my mom would beat her cancer.

Chapter 5

The day of my 18th birthday arrived, which meant summer was coming to an end soon. I had already registered for college and was looking forward to beginning my classes in the fall. Life was beginning to feel somewhat normal again. I woke up feeling blissful, knowing that although the year had been rough, I was now back home. My mom got me a beautiful necklace as a gift, pink heart diamonds on a slim gold chain. Jane came over that evening to join in on singing me Happy Birthday and cutting me a cake. I found myself more appreciative of this tradition than ever before.

A few days later, I brought my mom to one of her routine doctor visits. When we got back home, Jane was there with my niece so we could all spend time together. *"I did it! I beat my cancer!"* my mom happily exclaimed to Jane and I. My niece was only nine months old, so she didn't quite understand what was going on, but she seemed equally as happy as we did to hear the good news. At times, perception can be even more important than the message itself.

My first day of college arrived, I had been dying for this day to come. I wasn't always a fan of school back in high school, but I truly believed college would be better. After all, I got to choose my classes and my area of study. What could possibly interfere?

Shortly after sitting down for orientation, Lucas walked into the room. He saw me at the same time and, without hesitation, sat down next to me. *"I miss you."* He said as I looked over at him. I had honestly enjoyed our time apart, but Lucas had been one of my good friends even prior to our dating, so I understood. *"We can hang out when this is over,"* I told him in response. We took the train together once orientation finished, and I listened to Lucas tell me all the reasons why we should get back together. I was indifferent.

The next morning I awoke at my usual time to get ready for classes, but the bathroom was already occupied. I knocked on the door, *"Mom? Are you ok?"* my mom hadn't been up early ever since she stopped working to begin her cancer treatments. *"I'll be out in a second, sweetie,"* she responded. She opened the door, not looking so great, so I grabbed her arm to help support her balance and walked her back to her bedroom. Moments after sitting at her bedside, she began to uncontrollably throw up all over. I didn't even have a chance to react when she collapsed to the floor and began seizing. This was her first seizure with me, but I had been previously prepared. I knew to just hold her as it passed. Despite her wishes, I called for an ambulance and hopped in behind the EMTs carrying her on the stretcher.

"I'm in so much pain," she groaned as she lay in the bed in the emergency room. I held her hand with one hand and

texted Jane with the other. *"I'm sorry, Mom. Jane is on her way to meet us here."* We were so confused about what was happening, considering she had just told us recently she beat her cancer. Once pain meds kicked in, she felt slightly better, *"I'm so sorry,"* she said to me. *"For what, Mom?"* I asked, *"You're my baby; I'm supposed to be taking care of you,"* she responded right before slipping into a coma.

Jane and I took turns watching my niece so that she could also spend time by my mom's bedside. We patiently awaited news that things would get better, but with every swap Jane and I made, another one of our mom's organs failed. *"Do you girls want to sign a DNR?"* the doctor asked us, *"We don't understand,"* I responded, *"Our mom said she had beat her cancer?"* The doctor, who had recently begun treating our mom again after her departure from NYU hospital and falling out with Edna, looked at us very puzzled. *"When I last saw your mother, I told her I didn't know how she was still walking around. Her original prognosis from a year ago was six months."* We stood there heartbroken and at a loss for words. We realized the doctors were only now letting us both be by her side simultaneously with my baby niece because they didn't believe our mom had much time left. Before we could even agree to sign a DNR, the machine let out an eerie beep; she was gone.

This wasn't the way we believed things would be; this definitely didn't go according to plan.

www.ingramcontent.com/pod-product-compliance
Lightning Source LLC
Chambersburg PA
CBHW050157130526
44590CB00044B/3372